Daddy's Little Girl

30-Day Devotional

Heidi Catherine Rabe

For my Heavenly Father,
You are dearly loved by Your little girl.

Introduction

When my dear cat passed away in 2008, I spent the next year studying God's love. It was during that year that I wrote the poem "Daddy's Little Girl." I tucked a copy of it away in a notebook and forgot about it until four years later. During those four years, my grandma passed away, and then my other cat, then my other grandma, my great-aunt, and then my mom. It was one loss right after another. I have learned that during times of loss, the Heavenly Father is especially near and dear. My hope is that this devotional will bring all who read it closer to the Heavenly Father.

I went through many old cards, letters, and notes after my mom passed away. She kept just about everything. I even found little poems I had scribbled as a child. I probably didn't know that they were poems at the time, but that's what they were. Recently, I was thinking about poetry in today's world. I was wondering if it is necessary. The Lord reminded me that there are many hardships in life. The kind of writing I do serves as a reminder that there are beautiful things around us. We just need to see them. The source of all beauty, of course, comes from God.

1. How does James 1:17 describe the gifts from above?

2. Who gives us these gifts?

3. The context of this verse points us to salvation. According to John 3:16, who did the Heavenly Father give us?

Jesus is the greatest gift because He gives us access to the Father in Heaven. Accepting Jesus as Savior and Lord is the first step. In Romans 10:9-10, it says, "If you declare with your mouth, 'Jesus is Lord,' and believe in your heart that God raised him from the dead, you will be saved. For it is with your heart that you believe and are justified, and it is with your mouth that you profess your faith and are saved."

When my husband and I minister to new Christians, we emphasize accepting Jesus as Savior. We believe He died for our sins and arose from the dead so we can have eternal life. From that moment on, we live the life He has given us through His Lordship. When we say, "Jesus is Lord," we proclaim that He is the Lord of our life, our day, our hopes, our dreams, our failures, our successes, difficult situations, happy moments, everything! His name is greater than all these things. He will be with us through it all.

If you have yet to receive Jesus as your Savior and Lord, and you would like to, this would be a good time. According to 2 Corinthians 6:2, today is the day of salvation. Please talk to Him from your heart. You may like to write a prayer on the next page.

Daddy's Little Girl

Daddy's little girl,
You are
I AM.
Daddy's little girl
who sits on a knee,
please read to me
about the stars in heaven's sky,
how you make the fishies swim,
the birdies fly,
how you never tell a lie.
You are the best Daddy
in my eyes.

No greater gift could there be
than to have You here with me.
Abba Father, Daddy, home,
in Your arms I'm not alone.
You whisper softly in my ear,
"I love you, daughter, child, My dear."
Abba Father, Daddy's girl,
You make me glisten in this world.

I'm just Daddy's little girl
right now,
right here,
Daddy's little girl
held so close, so dear.
You wipe away my tears.
You make me giggle in the rain,
draw the sunshine in the clouds
and feel my every pain.
I crawl upon your knee again
and again and again,
my best friend.

Daddy's little girl,
so big,
so brave,
Daddy's little girl,
I can walk and run and play
while You create the day.
You hold the hours in Your palm,
paint a rainbow with Your hand
and cause the seas to calm.
You tell me when things are done.
You are the best Daddy.
I am your psalm.

Day 1

Daddy's Little Girl

When you look at the life of Jesus, it is remarkable to see His heart for children. In Matthew 18:1-5, His disciples ask, "Who is the greatest in the kingdom of heaven?" If you have read this story before, you probably remember that Jesus calls a little child. He tells His disciples that "unless you change and become like little children, you will never enter the kingdom of heaven. Therefore, whoever takes the lowly position of this child is the greatest in the kingdom of heaven. And whoever welcomes one such child in my name welcomes me."

I have met a number of deep thinkers during my Christian walk. If I were to ask you to describe what a philosopher looks like, you might say that he is old with a long beard and perhaps glasses. You may think of Aristotle or one of the other great Greek philosophers. Oftentimes people come to God with complex thoughts of life. My husband asked me recently, "How do we know if we are on the narrow road?" I thought for a moment, and then I said, "God isn't looking for a perfected philosopher with a beard and glasses. He just wants us to come to Him as little children through faith in Christ."

According to the Strong's Concordance, the word "narrow" involves trouble or suffering (most likely for the sake of the gospel). As children of God, we will certainly face persecution and hardship. But, thank the Lord, He is with us.

So, getting back to the Bible story, we can see that it takes a place of humility for someone to admit that they need God. Notice how Jesus calls the little child, and then the child comes to Him. The verse doesn't say if the child is a little boy or a little girl. I like to think that gender isn't included so that each one of us, whether male or female, will be able to relate to the child. In order to enter the kingdom of heaven, we must become like little children. We must come to God when He calls.

1. According to Galatians 3:26, how do we become children of God?

You may not have godly parents, or perhaps you don't have parents at all. Perhaps you feel disconnected from God even though you believe in Him. A good place to begin is to embrace your Heavenly Father through faith. Believe He is there for you even if you do not feel that way. One helpful thing to do is to keep a journal. Write down moments you have with the Lord. It could be a verse that applies to your day. It could be a way that God has provided for you. It could even be the beauty of the sunrise or sunset. Begin to take note of God. He takes note of you!

2. Please write your name on the line below.

The Lord watches over

_____.

"Enter through the narrow gate. For wide is the gate and broad is the road that leads to destruction, and many enter through it. But small is the gate and narrow the road that leads to life, and only a few find it."

Matthew 7:13-14

Day 2

You are I AM

When I first wrote "Daddy's Little Girl," the punctuation went something like this:

Daddy's little girl,

you are,

I am

Daddy's little girl

who sits on a knee...

As I wrote the first few words of the poem, I thought I was speaking to another female. We are both Daddy's little girls. You are Daddy's little girl just like I am Daddy's little girl.

When I discovered the poem in a notebook four years later, I read it in a brand-new way. This is what I suddenly saw:

Daddy's little girl,

You are

I AM.

Daddy's little girl

who sits on a knee...

Do you happen to see the difference? I know it is a very slight difference, but it makes a really big difference. In this version, the little girl is speaking to God. She is saying, "You are I AM."

1. Please take a moment to read Exodus 3:11-14.

In Exodus 3:11, Moses says to God, "Who am I that I should go to Pharaoh and bring the Israelites out of Egypt?" So often we are concerned with ourselves. Who am I? How could I possibly do this or that? But God reassures Moses that He will be with him. The focus switches from "who am I" to the great "I AM." In verse 14, God says to Moses, "I AM WHO I AM. This is what you are to say to the Israelites: 'I AM has sent me to you.'" And I AM will be with you too!

2. What is your greatest need at this time? Fill in the blank with a word that describes how God is there for you.

I AM your

_____.

3. In the Gospel of John, Jesus repeats the phrase "I am" seven times. Once you look up the verses, please fill in each blank.

a) "I am the _____ of life" (John 6:35).

b) "I am the _____ of the world" (John 8:12).

c) "I am the _____" (John 10:9).

d) "I am the _____ _____" (John 10:11).

e) "I am the _____ and the _____" (John 11:25).

f) "I am the _____, the _____, and the _____" (John 14:6).

g) "I am the _____" (John 15:5).

Day 3

Sit on a Knee

When I think about a young child on her daddy's knee, I imagine that she runs over to him and jumps in his lap. Even a timid child would know her daddy's love and embrace the moment with confidence and joy.

Even though we can't physically sit on our Heavenly Father's knee, we can know where we are seated (spiritually speaking, of course).

1. According to Ephesians 1:20, where is Christ seated?

2. Please read Ephesians 2:6. Where are you seated?

The Greek word for "sit" in Ephesians 2:6 is *sugkathizo*. It means "to give (or take) a seat in company with" and "to (make) sit (down) together." Its root word speaks of "union." We could also think of it as communion. There is a closeness that we share with the Lord when we sit with Him. And one day we will have the opportunity to sit with Him in His kingdom, probably at the marriage supper of the Lamb.

The story about Martha and Mary suddenly comes to mind. In Luke 10:38-42, the younger sister, Mary, decides to sit at Jesus' feet. If she had been a little child, she may have sat on a knee. Being a grown-up, however, Mary chooses a humble, yet personal place by His feet. Martha, the older sister, is concerned about Mary's choice. She feels her little sister should help with domestic things instead of sitting with the Lord. Jesus, however, tells Martha that Mary has chosen what is better. Both activities are good, but one was (and is) definitely better. Sitting with the Lord and listening to Him would not be taken away from Mary.

3. Do you relate better to Martha or Mary? Why?

4. Where is your favorite place to spend time with the Lord?

"God is spirit, and his worshipers must worship in the Spirit and in truth."

John 4:24

Day 4

Please Read to Me

I love it when someone reads to me. It's probably one of my favorite things. I remember back in fifth grade when our teacher read *From the Mixed-Up Files of Mrs. Basil E. Frankweiler* by E. L. Konigsburg. She read it out loud to our class. It's the only time I recall being read to as a child, although I'm sure there were other times. I soaked up every word and never wanted it to end.

Every now and then my husband, Kirk, will read me a story. Every Christmas I look forward to *Song of the Stars* by Sally Lloyd-Jones. For my birthday he reads one of the tales from *Frog and Toad are Friends* by Arnold Lobel. And every time we read the Bible, our Heavenly Father tells us His story.

1. According to 2 Timothy 3:16, how much Scripture is God-breathed? Circle one.

      Some   **Most**   **All**

2. There are four ways we can use Scripture. You will find the answers in 2 Timothy 3:16. Please write them below.

a)

b)

c)

d)

The Bible is filled with true stories about people who were led by God, touched by Him, and changed by Him in amazing ways. It is a privilege to have the freedom to read and study the Word. Not everyone has had this opportunity.

3. Write your favorite verse below.

4. Which story from the Bible do you like the best?

I had to really think before I finally narrowed my favorite Bible stories down to two. There are so many good ones! One of my favorites is the Christmas story. I didn't grow up hearing a lot of Bible stories, but I knew about the birth of Jesus. To think that He was a little baby born in a stable, perhaps even surrounded by little animals, brings me so much joy! Everyone loves babies. And babies grow into children. Luke 2:52 says that "Jesus grew in wisdom and stature, and in favor with God and man."

5. What did Jesus say to His parents when they found Him in the temple? You will find the answer in Luke 2:49.

Day 5

Stars in Heaven's Sky

Genesis 1:16 tells us that God made the stars. People sometimes wonder how the God of the universe has time to look after, what they consider to be, their small and insignificant lives. I'd like to take a look at it from a different perspective. To me, it seems that if God is able to create and care for the stars, He most certainly is able to care for you and me. When I look at the night sky and see the moon and the stars, I am amazed that God not only made them, but that He set them in the sky.

1. According to Genesis 1:17, which planet benefits from the stars?

2. How do the stars help the earth?

God cares for us so much that He made the stars to give us light at night. Kirk and I live in a neighborhood that doesn't have streetlights. For the first time in my life, I've had to rely on the moon and the stars for light. I am very grateful for a clear night when the stars are especially bright.

3. Psalm 147:4 tells us two things about the stars. Write each one below.

a)

b)

When you attend a church service, are you able to name each adult, teenager, child, and baby? If you are a part of smaller congregation, you may actually answer "yes." Most people, however, probably wouldn't be able to name every person. Now add all the stars in the sky to your list. How many stars can you name? To think that God not only knows how many stars exist, but He calls each one of them by name! If we could hear Him tell a story about all the stars in Heaven's sky, I'm sure we would be captivated and amazed. Thankfully, we have the Bible to tell us what we need to know for now.

"Lift up your eyes and look to the heavens: Who created all these? He who brings out the starry host one by one and calls forth each of them by name. Because of his great power and mighty strength, not one of them is missing."

Isaiah 40:26

4. Lift up your eyes to the starry sky tonight. Say a prayer to your Heavenly Father. Thank Him for His light.

"God is more glorious than the moon; he shines brighter than the stars."

Job 25:5 (NLT)

Day 6

Fishies Swim

After God made the stars, the Bible tells us that He created the fish and the birds. Genesis 1:20 says, "Let the water teem with living creatures, and let birds fly above the earth across the vault of the sky." Today we are going to take a look at a story in the Bible involving fish. We will, therefore, have to place each bird in its nest until tomorrow.

The Sea of Galilee was a popular fishing hole during Bible times. When I visited the sea, I was surprised by its size. It was more like a big lake. In fact, Luke 5:1 calls it the "Lake of Gennesaret," which happens to be another name for the Sea of Galilee. In this story, the people are crowding around Jesus to hear Him teach. Therefore, Jesus gets into one of the boats on shore.

1. Read Luke 5:3. Who owns the boat?

2. According to verse 5, how many fish did Simon Peter's crew catch during the night shift. Circle one.

100   **50**   **0**

In verse 4, Jesus tells Peter to take the boat out into deep water. He is supposed to let down the nets for a catch. After a whole night of not catching one single fish, I'm sure Peter wonders if it is worth the trouble to try again. But he obeys what the Lord tells him to do. Verse 6 explains that they catch so many fish that their nets begin to break!

3. Why do you suppose they caught fish this time?

4. I think the answer to question 3 can be summed up with the following verse. Please fill in the blanks.

"The earth is the _____, and _____ in it...."

Psalm 24:1

Simply put, Jesus is Lord of all creation. Fish are a part of God's creation. I believe God guided each fish into Peter's net. Peter obeyed. The fish obeyed. And just look at those fishies swim!

Consider all of creation. Jesus is Lord over the stars, the fish, the birds, the wind, and the sea. And He is Lord over you and me.

"What kind of man is this? Even the winds and the waves obey him!"

Matthew 8:27

Day 7

Birdies Fly

"Look at the birds of the air; they do not sow or reap or store away in barns, and yet your heavenly Father feeds them. Are you not much more valuable than they?"

Matthew 6:26

Throughout the years, I've heard an occasional "thump" when a bird hits one of our windows. Usually it's the bay window on the backside of our house. So, we've placed stickers on all the windows, which has helped. And recently we built a large feeder, as well as a garden, in the backyard. Since then, only about one or two birds have grazed the windows. Thankfully, those things seem to be helping.

One day, a few months ago, Kirk and I heard a loud "thump" in the kitchen. I knew right then and there that it was a bird. Kirk hadn't seen a fallen bird before. He wondered if we should go outside and help it. I said it was better to stay inside and pray for her from the other side of the window. I didn't want to upset the little cardinal since she was already dazed and confused. I thought we may do more harm than good. I told Kirk that I would pray for the little bird. She would eventually roll onto her side, her belly, and then fly into a shrub nearby. Kirk said, "How do you know?" I explained that I've been through this process before. So, I sat on the bench and prayed for the next 30 minutes. During that time, the cardinal rolled onto her side, her belly, and then flew into a shrub where she sat for about another hour.

So, why do I care about the birds? Well, because God cares. According to Matthew 10:29, God knows when a sparrow falls to the ground.

1. Fill in the blanks for the verse below.

"So don't be _____; you are worth _____ than many sparrows."

Matthew 10:31

Matthew 10:29 tells us that two sparrows were sold for a penny during Bible times. Well, aren't you glad to know that you're worth more than a penny? I'm just kidding. I don't think God's point here is the monetary value of birds. He is trying to teach us about His love and care for the birds. When we finally understand that our Heavenly Father cares for these tiny creatures, then perhaps we will begin to understand that He cares for us too.

One reason I love poetry is because it is about the little things. There aren't too many living things that are smaller than birds. Remember that God cares for the little things, whether it's the little details of your life or the little creatures in your backyard. I've often said that He is God of the big picture as well as God of the details.

2. If you have any cares, please write them below.

3. Take a moment to pray to your Heavenly Father. Cast all your cares on Him because He cares for you (1 Peter 5:7).

Day 8

Never Tell a Lie

David was many things throughout his life: a shepherd boy, a king, a musician, a psalmist, and a man after God's own heart (just to name a few). The psalms that David penned help us understand the ups and downs that he faced as king of Israel. His writings also help us see that he was a man who needed and desired God.

1. David wrote Psalm 25. Please fill in the blanks for verse 5.

"_____ me in your _____ and

_____ me, for you are God my Savior, and my

_____ is in you all day long."

Psalm 25:5

Let's take a look at the first part of this verse. It says, "Guide me in your truth...."

2. Who is David speaking to in Psalm 25? You will find the answer in verse 1.

David is asking God to guide him in His truth.

Numbers 23:19 explains that "God is not a man, that he should lie" (KJV). Some people think a little "white lie" is okay. This is a lie that is told to avoid hurting someone's feelings. But God is incapable of any kind of lying, whether it is white, black, red, pink, or green.

3. How does Jesus describe the Word in John 17:17?

Every time we read the Bible, we read the truth. Isn't it refreshing to know that we can know the truth? There are many difficulties, even lies, that could bring us down each day. God's truth, however, will guide us, teach us, and bring us hope all day long.

"To the Jews who had believed him, Jesus said, 'If you hold to my teaching, you are really my disciples. Then you will know the truth, and the truth will set you free.'"

John 8:31

4. Finish today's lesson by thanking God for the truth of His Word. You may want to write a prayer below.

Day 9

In My Eyes

"I love the Lord, for he heard my voice; he heard my cry for mercy. Because he turned his ear to me, I will call on him as long as I live."

Psalm 116:1-2

Throughout the Bible, we read stories about people who were rescued or healed in miraculous ways. Sometimes it takes years—often many, many years—of walking with God to have a collection of memories of times when He intervened on your behalf. It takes time to develop a relationship with God, to know when He's speaking to you, to know when He's guiding you, to have no doubt that He's there for you, to know that you can call on Him anytime and anyplace.

1. Please write down a time when your Heavenly Father intervened on your behalf.

As I already mentioned, I've been through many losses in recent years. The most difficult one was the loss of my mom. The Lord immediately stepped in to help me with practical everyday things. During a two year period, His presence was so strong in ways I had never experienced before. As He comforted my soul, the revelation of God as my Heavenly Father became ever so dear.

I now read Psalm 116:1-2 with confidence that my Heavenly Father is there for me, and I will look to Him as long as I live.

2. Name three ways you can look to God.

    a)

    b)

    c)

3. What does God mean to you?

There are many things that can take our eyes off the Lord. They can, in a way, become little idols in our lives. The very first of the Ten Commandments says, "You shall have no other gods before me." You'll find a list of the Ten Commandments in Exodus 20:1-17. An idol doesn't have to be a statue set on a mantle with candles around it, although I suppose it could be. Idols, in our day and age, could very easily be people, music, technology, hobbies, ideas, or pretty much anything that would take the place in our hearts and minds where only God should be.

What is so wonderful about God is that He knows us better than we know ourselves. He was aware of any idol long before you and I ever were. As we place God in the number one spot in our lives, things will start to make sense. He wants to be the best in our eyes, and rightfully so, because He is the best! One verse in the poem "Daddy's Little Girl" says, "You are the best Daddy in my eyes." Let this be your meditation for the day: My Heavenly Father is the best! I love Him more than anything.

"With whom, then, will you compare God?"

Isaiah 40:18

Day 10

No Greater Gift

1. Which Bible verse do you think is the most well-known?

My guess would be John 3:16. Perhaps you can recite this verse from memory. My Bible, which is the New International Version, says, "For God so loved the world that he gave his one and only Son, that whoever believes in him shall not perish but have eternal life."

2. According to John 3:16, who did God give us?

There is no greater gift than Jesus! Through Him we have forgiveness of sins. We also have access to our Father in Heaven.

3. Please take a moment to thank your Heavenly Father for His Son, Jesus.

4. Next, look up Mark 16:19. Where is Jesus seated?

(Please remember this position as we take a look at Psalm 16:11.)

"You make known to me the path of life; you will fill me with joy in your presence, with eternal pleasures at your right hand."

Psalm 16:11

Let's take a look at the first part of this verse. It says, "You make known to me the path of life." Of course, we know the path of life begins with Jesus. We start on this path the day we accept Him as Savior and Lord. (If this is something you would like to do, please take a moment to read the introduction at the beginning of this study.)

The next part of Psalm 16:11 says, "You will fill me with joy in your presence...." To me, there is nothing more precious than God's Word and His presence. Oftentimes people ask God to do things for them, which is important. But they often miss the greater blessing, which is simply being with God. I heard someone say that we're human beings, not human doings. Still, we are easily drawn to "doing" things. Of course, we have been created for good works (Ephesians 2:10). It is God's will that our lives reflect His goodness.

In recent years, I have finally reached a place in my walk with God where the "being" part has become more important than anything. I want to be with the Lord more than anything. I love to spend time with Him in Word, in prayer, in song. And, yes, like the Scripture says, there is fullness of joy.

The last part of the verse says, "with eternal pleasures at your right hand." We already learned who is seated at the right hand of God. It's Jesus!

5. How can you spend time with the Lord today?

Day 11

Abba Father

There is some debate over the meaning of the word "abba." Some scholars believe that it is a term of respect used to address older men and teachers. Other people emphasize the family unit where sons and daughters use this name to refer to their father throughout their lives. Then there are those who feel it is a term of tender endearment that a young child uses to call his or her daddy.

I'm a simple student of the Bible, and, of course, a child of God. In this study, I have chosen to look at the word "abba" from a child's point of view. It is, of course, only one possible interpretation. There is so much to learn as God's children. It is wise, I believe, to begin to see Him repectfully through the eyes of a child.

1. Romans 8:15 explains that we have been adopted as sons [and daughters]. What do we cry?

The name "Abba, Father" reveals as much about His children as it does the Father Himself. As we grow older, it is easy to see ourselves as self-sufficient. The younger a child happens to be, however, the more she will rely on her parents. As we approach our Heavenly Father as little children, we will begin to depend on Him more and more. It doesn't have to be an issue of pride or disrespect. Rather, when done with pure intentions, it will most certainly take a humble person to become as a little child. It isn't an invitation to act immature, or to become lazy or disobedient. Quite the contrary, it is an opportunity to draw close to the Heavenly Father and obey Him. It is a place to simply love Him.

"Follow God's example, therefore, as dearly loved children and walk in the way of love, just as Christ loved us and gave himself up for us as a fragrant offering and sacrifice to God."

Ephesians 5:1-2

Whenever I think about my mom and dad, I think of home. My earliest memory dates back to when I was about two and a half years old. We had just moved into our house in Richfield, Minnesota. My parents were painting our garage while I sat on a patio chair with my stuffed animals. One of the stuffed animals was a dog that belonged to my dad when he was little. Some of the white paint somehow got on the dog's leg. That's about all I remember.

When I think about my Heavenly Father, I imagine my eternal home in Heaven. Heaven is special for one very special reason: God is there. If Heaven weren't God's home, I don't think we would long for it as much. It's kind of like when I think back to my parents' home, I remember it was special because they were there.

We learn something very important about our eternal home in the Gospel of John. After Jesus tells His disciples He will only be with them a little longer, their hearts are troubled. Jesus then comforts them with some words.

2. Whose house does Jesus describe in John 14:2?

3. What does Jesus say He will do in John 14:3?

Day 12

In Your Arms

To me, there is nothing more comforting than the thought of being in my Heavenly Father's arms. And there is nothing more terrifying than the thought of not being with Him. I don't understand how people can make it through life without God. I'm not talking about going to church once a week or saying an occasional prayer. I'm talking about God being near and dear every moment of the day. There are so many challenges in life. I couldn't imagine having to face a difficulty without Him.

1. How has God helped you when you've been tempted to fear?

"So do not fear, for I am with you; do not be dismayed, for I am your God. I will strengthen you and help you; I will uphold you with my righteous right hand."

Isaiah 41:10

The best place to find strength, whether you're afraid or not, is with God. Study His Word. Pray without ceasing. Sing songs to the Lord. Make a joyful noise! He is there for you. He is with you. He will listen. Find rest in His arms.

Psalm 91 is one of my favorites. When I was young in the Lord, I took a class at church where we memorized this psalm. One part that is particularly fitting for today's study is verse 4. It says, "He will cover you with his feathers, and under his wings you will find refuge." I've heard stories about birds that have protected their young from fires. The little chicks remained safe under their mom's wings while the mom took the heat, so to speak. This is the way it is for you and me. We are safe under the shelter of our Heavenly Father's wings. He will watch over us during any storm.

2. **Please take a few minutes to memorize Psalm 91:4. It is written below.**

"He will cover you with his feathers, and under his wings you will find refuge."

Psalm 91:4

3. **Even though you may want to skip over this activity, take a moment to "curl up" in your Heavenly Father's arms. Express your thoughts about His protection and care over your life.**

Day 13

Whisper Softly

The main way God speaks to us is through His written Word, which is the Bible. Whatever God speaks to us will always line up with Scripture.

1. How does Hebrews 4:12 describe the Word of God? Try to list five things.

    a)

    b)

    c)

    d)

    e)

Elijah was on the run. He was the only prophet left, and people were trying to kill him. First Kings 19:11 tells us that the Lord said, "Go out and stand on the mountain in the presence of the Lord, for the Lord is about to pass by."

2. If you were about to experience God's presence, how do you imagine He would reveal Himself to you?

Verse 11 describes a great and powerful wind that tore the mountains apart and shattered the rocks.

3. According to 1 Kings 19:11, was the Lord in the wind?

Yes   No

4. After the wind, there was an earthquake. Was the Lord in the earthquake?

Yes   No

Things have really been shaken up by this time. You would think this would be enough, but verse 12 tells us that after the earthquake came a fire.

5. Was the Lord in the fire?

Yes   No

Elijah must have wondered what on earth was next. There had been wind, mountains falling apart, shattered rocks, an earthquake, and then a fire. It sounds like a pretty rough day. We've all had one of those days in one way or another. When earth-shattering days happen, there is one thing that we desperately need. We need to hear from God.

6. According to 1 Kings 19:12, what came after the fire?

God will sometimes speak to us through a gentle whisper, often called a still small voice. This whisper isn't an audible voice, but it does always line up with the Word of God.

Day 14

I Love You

I am convinced that there is nothing more important than knowing God loves you. "For God so loved the world that he gave his one and only Son...." Most problems in life, I believe, stem from a lack of understanding of God's love. Perhaps one of the most important years of my life was spent studying the love of God. I recommend it for everyone. Of course, it's important to be led by the Holy Spirit as to what He would have you read. Not every book on love is from God. The Bible is the best source!

When I thought about stories in the Word of God that demonstrate our Heavenly Father's love, I immediately thought of the prodigal son. The man in the story represents our Heavenly Father. The older son represents the Pharisees and the teachers of the Law, while the younger represents the son who strayed.

1. According to Luke 15:13, what did the younger son do?

The younger son spent everything. He eventually ended up getting a job feeding pigs. As he looked at the pods that the pigs were eating, he wanted some too. He had reached his lowest point.

2. Read Luke 15:17. Who had food?

The prodigal son decided he would go back to his father and say to him:

"Father, I have sinned against heaven and against you. I am no longer worthy to be called your son; make me like one of your hired servants."

Luke 15:18-19

If I may quote Dorothy from *The Wizard of Oz*: "There's no place like home." The younger son finally realized that his father's house was better than anything the world could offer.

3. When did his father see him? You will find the answer in Luke 15:20.

Don't you just love that? His father must have been looking for him. He had been waiting for this day. He was filled with compassion for his lost son. In fact, he ran to his son, and then he hugged him and kissed him. He loved him. And your Heavenly Father loves you!

"The father said to his servants, 'Quick! Bring the best robe and put it on him. Put a ring on his finger and sandals on his feet. Bring the fatted calf and kill it. Let's have a feast and celebrate. For this son of mine was dead and is alive again; he was lost and is found.'"

Luke 15:22-24

Day 15

You Make Me Glisten

It has been several weeks since I've had an opportunity to write. Kirk's parents were here for a visit. Then my dad stayed during Thanksgiving week. Last week my cat, Katarina, had surgery. Today, thankfully, she is finally resting well. Right now she is curled up next to me on her favorite blanket. Oh, what a special day!

1. How is today special to you?

During the last month or so, I've been thinking about what I should write for today's devotion. Then it occurred to me that Hanukkah begins this evening. How exciting! Ever since I returned from Israel, I've been fascinated with the temple. Hanukkah is a time to remember how God made a one-day supply of oil for the temple's menorah burn for eight days. During Jesus' time, Hanukkah was known as the Feast (or Festival) of Dedication. It is still called by this name today.

2. Please read John 10:22-23. Where was Jesus during the Festival of Dedication?

I love that Jesus was in the temple during this celebration!

3. How does Jesus describe Himself in John 8:12?

The light of the world was celebrating the light in the temple. How amazing is that! The holy place in the temple would have been dark without the light from the lampstand. Just a side note: The Festival of Dedication is also called the Festival of Lights.

4. During the Sermon on the Mount, Jesus mentions light. What does He tell His disciples in Matthew 5:14?

Jesus is the source of light. As His followers, we reflect His light in a dark world. We glisten! Light provides illumination. It also guides. Have you ever tried to find your way in the dark? If so, then you know how difficult it can be. Many people are trying to find their way through spiritual darkness. As we point people to Jesus, the Holy Spirit will illuminate the Word and guide people into all truth.

Jesus said, "But when he, the Spirit of truth, comes, he will guide you into all the truth."

John 16:13

Day 16

Here & Now

As a poet, perhaps the most important thing is to live in the moment. I remember when social media was first introduced to me. A shift took place. On one hand, a part of me liked it (for a season). On the other hand, I longed for the way things used to be. My focus was pulled away from the moment, from the here and now, from the world around me, and ultimately from God. My thoughts used to be filled with the next Bible study, but suddenly I seemed more concerned with what so-and-so was doing somewhere else. I often regret ever becoming a part of the social media world.

Since then, I have cut it out of my life pretty well. I am almost back to the place where I used to be. When I get up in the morning, my thoughts are filled with the Lord. I have a routine where I feed the animals. It is my favorite time of day as I sing songs to the Lord. Hours will go by where I don't even consider what so-and-so is doing over here or over there. Of course, other people's lives are important. But the point is that no one is more important than God. He should be our song in the morning, our companion throughout the day, our rest for the night. He should be our everything! The Lord deserves a place of honor and love.

I am grateful to be back in a place of the here and now. I enjoy life more. I appreciate the world around me. I think about God more. And I am happy to be His little girl.

1. Please write Psalm 96:4 below.

The Lord is great! This truth alone is more than enough reason to give Him our best. Psalm 96:4 goes on to say that He is most worthy of praise. There are people or things which are acknowledged from time to time, but only God is most worthy. He is the only one who is worthy of our praise.

2. How would you describe "praise"?

Before the fall, Adam and Eve had everything they could ever want or need. They had perfect fellowship with the Lord. They had one another. They ruled over amazing animals. There was an abundance of nutritious food. Plus, it was a beautiful place to live. Within this perfection, however, they still felt that something was lacking. Adam and Eve felt like they were missing out on something. I believe this is the root of the problem. This is the reason why they left their first love.

Modern-day Christians sometimes feel like they are missing out as well. Some may feel like they are missing out on the latest phone, the latest music, or perhaps the latest kind of church. Like King Solomon said, "What has been will be again, what had been done will be done again; there is nothing new under the sun" (Ecclesiastes 1:9). We all have a tendency to want a little more. It just happens to get packaged a little differently from generation to generation.

3. Name one thing you could set aside to spend more time with God.

Day 17

Close & Dear

Our walk with God begins with faith. One of my teachers often told our class that "faith is simply believing." Sometimes even the thought that God is with us has to be embraced by faith. There may be times when we feel all alone, but God is always there.

1. Please take a moment to read Psalm 34:18. Where is God in this verse?

"Brokenhearted" means grievously sad. It is when you're filled with great sadness because someone you love has left you or died. I have come to know being brokenhearted all too well during the last several years.

2. Have you ever been brokenhearted? If so, you may want to write about it below.

The next part of the poem I've written says:

Daddy's little girl,

held so close,

so dear...

Our Heavenly Father holds us close in a spiritual sense. We are dear to Him. You are dear to Him. In Hebrews 13:5, God says, "Never will I leave you; never will I forsake you."

King David writes about God's presence in Psalm 139:7-10. He says, "Where can I go from your Spirit? Where can I flee from your presence? If I go up to the heavens, you are there; if I make my bed in the depths, you are there. If I rise on the wings of the dawn, if I settle on the far side of the sea, even there your hand will guide me, your right hand will hold me fast."

3. Which verse speaks to you most personally concerning God's presence in your life? It could be a verse we've already discussed or perhaps a new one.

"The Lord is close to the brokenhearted
and saves those who are crushed in spirit."

Psalm 34:18

Day 18

My Tears

One of my favorite verses in the Bible has to do with prayer. In Revelation 5:8, it says that "the four living creatures and the twenty-four elders fell down before the Lamb. Each one had a harp and they were holding golden bowls full of incense...."

1. What are the golden bowls full of incense? See Revelation 5:8.

To think that God keeps our prayers in golden bowls in Heaven is quite an amazing thought. What we say to God is important to Him. God hears our prayers. And He keeps them in a very special place.

There is something else that God keeps.

2. Please read Psalm 56:8. What did you discover God keeps?

The New Living Translation says:

"You keep track of all my sorrows. You have collected all my tears in your bottle. You have recorded each one in your book."

Psalm 56:8

3. How many of your tears has God collected? Circle one.

A few   **Some**   **All**

From the time you are born until the time you die, God keeps track of every single sorrow. There are probably tears that we have long forgotten, but God never forgets. He remembers each one.

4. What do you keep in a bowl around your home? You may like to draw a picture of it below.

5. What do you keep in a bottle?

God's golden bowls are filled with your prayers. His bottle is filled with your tears. How precious is that! Please remember these things as you speak with Him today.

Day 19

Giggle in the Rain

One afternoon I stood with a couple of women near a doorway. We watched as it rained outside. None of us had an umbrella, so we were left with one of two options: wait it out or run like the wind. One by one we made a mad dash, each one heading to her own car. You could hear the giggles, the laughter. We didn't want to get wet, and yet it seemed to bring a childlike joy to each one of us.

1. Think of a time you experienced childlike joy.

When I was little, I loved to go out in the rain with my colorful umbrella. I would mimic Gene Kelly in *Singing in the Rain*, jumping in puddles, twirling the umbrella, splashing around, and, of course, singing. But life happens. A gentle rain can quickly turn into a severe storm. A tornado can seem to devastate all the life around us as well as within us.

2. How do you hold on to joy during a stormy season?

The joy of the Lord doesn't necessarily involve laughter, although it may at times. Rather, it often comes to bring relief from trials. The biblical definition of "joy" could be any of the following, depending on the context: rejoicing, gladness, cheerfulness, relief, or calm delight.

3. Which of the words above speaks the most to you right now? Why?

I have experienced the Lord's joy during the most difficult times of my life. Looking at the circumstances, I shouldn't have been joyful at all, but I was. I know it had to be the fruit of the Spirit, as well as God's grace.

4. Please take a moment to write down all nine of the fruit of the Spirit. You will find them in Galatians 5:22-23.

"The Lord is my strength and my shield; my heart trusts in him, and he helps me. My heart leaps for joy, and with my song I praise him."

Psalm 28:7

If you happen to encounter a storm today, whether it is in the form of droplets from the sky or tears from your eyes, just know that the Lord's joy will bring you strength. Sing Him a song in the rain.

Day 20

Sunshine in the Clouds

"Every cloud has a silver lining" is a phrase that was inspired by a poem called "Comus: A Mask Presented at Ludlow Castle, 1634" by John Milton. The phrase is a reminder that every bad situation (the cloud) has something good (a silver lining).

1. Write down something good that came out of a difficult time in your life.

There is a blessing that the Lord told Moses to share with Aaron and his sons. It was a blessing that the priests would pray over the Israelites. It is special to me since my mom used to say it frequently.

"The Lord bless you and keep you;
the Lord make his face shine on you and be gracious to you;
the Lord turn his face toward you and give you peace."

Numbers 6:24-26

2. Which part of Numbers 6:24-26 do you like the best?

Since the title of today's devotion is "Sunshine in the Clouds," we will focus on verse 25. It begins by saying may "the Lord make his face shine on you…."

3. When the Lord's face shines on you, what are the benefits?
   See Numbers 6:24-26.

Of course, the most obvious sunshine in the Bible is the Son of God. He is the silver lining in a dark and dying world. He is the Son-shine of our lives!

4. How does God's Son bring peace to your life?

Day 21

Every Pain

One particular verse comes to mind concerning how God feels about our pain:

"For we do not have a high priest who is unable to empathize with our weaknesses, but we have one who has been tempted in every way, just as we are—yet he did not sin."

Hebrews 4:15

Jesus is the High Priest who is able to relate to our weaknesses since He, too, was human. He knows how we feel. He understands our struggles. He even experienced temptation.

1. Please read Hebrews 4:15 and then fill in the blank.

Jesus was tempted, yet He did not _____.

Jesus was 100% man and 100% God. He lived life in a body, and He is the only one who has ever lived life perfectly. He was without sin.

2. Why did God send His Son into the world? See John 3:17.

When you come to God with a pain or struggle, He will not condemn you. He sent His Son to save you. Through Christ we find comfort, peace, forgiveness, love, and the list goes on and on.

3. What does the first part of Isaiah 53:4 say?

This is a prophecy about Jesus' death on the cross. It says He took our pain and bore our suffering. In the depths of pain, Jesus understands. In the fragility of brokenness, He restores. In the midst of any weakness, He empathizes.

4. How can Jesus relate to a painful time in your life?

Day 22

Best Friend

The world of a little child is usually limited to her parents and perhaps a sibling or two. If you asked her to draw a picture of her best friend, you would likely see a smiling portrait of her mommy or daddy. As we get older, however, friendships expand to cousins, classmates, teammates, and neighbors. Our world continues to grow. Social media is a good example of this. Suddenly, you may appear to have 200 friends or followers. How about that! We work so hard to build this network of people around us, and yet we've lost our first love.

1. Which church lost its first love? See Revelation 2:1,4.

2. What did Jesus say is the greatest commandment? You will find the answer in Matthew 22:37-38.

To live as God's little children we must first put our relationships in order, not neglect them or ignore them, but rather understand their place in light of God's place in our lives. As His little child, your Heavenly Father becomes your world, your best friend. A little child thinks of her parents regularly. She runs to her mommy or daddy for a hug, for comfort, for food, for love.

3. **We grow up naturally and spiritually, and yet we can always approach our Heavenly Father as His little child. What thoughts do you have about this statement?**

You may think this is good in theory, but how do we put it into practice?

4. **Please write 1 John 4:19 below.**

The more you understand how much God loves you, the easier it will become to live life as His little child. Children weren't respected during Bible times. Even the disciples thought the children were bothering Jesus.

5. **Read Matthew 9:13-15. How did Jesus feel about children?**

Jesus came to do His Father's will (John 6:38). He said, "Anyone who has seen me has seen the Father" (14:9). Since Jesus loves the little children, then we know that the Heavenly Father loves them too (regardless of their age).

Day 23

Big & Brave

It was the Easter season. I was about three years old—Mom's little helper as we searched for decorations in the basement. There was a big bunny candle that looked like chocolate. I wanted to carry that bunny up the stairs more than anything. Mom explained that it was too heavy and that I may drop it. I was determined to carry that bunny, though. I was a big girl... and so brave! I got about half way up the stairs when the bunny fell out of my little arms and tumbled down with a thump, thump, thump (a sound that bunnies often make, but not usually this way). Both ears had broken. I hurried down the stairs and sat by the pieces with tears flowing down my cheeks. Mom said, "Don't worry. We will fix him." She then glued each ear, securing them on his head. I can say with much relief that the bunny made his way to our table for many, many years to come (battle scars and all).

1. Recall a brave moment in your life.

Little children are perhaps the bravest people. They have to learn things and do things for the very first time. As they take their first step, they fall down, yet they get back up and try again.

I am sure that I wouldn't have attempted to carry the bunny had my mom not been with me. Perhaps I was doing it to show her that I could do it. Being the youngest, I was always trying to keep up with the big kids. I wanted to be big too. I wanted to do big people things...like carry bunnies.

"Be strong and courageous. Do not be afraid or terrified because of them, for the Lord your God goes with you; he will never leave you nor forsake you."

Deuteronomy 31:6

2. In Deuteronomy 31:6, Moses reassures the Israelites that God is with them. Which part of this verse speaks to your present situation?

God goes with us through every situation, whether good or bad. When I carried the bunny up the stairs, my mom was with me. She knew the bunny or I may fall, so she was right there to help. Just like God was with the Israelites as they stepped out into unknown territory, so God is with us. We should not be afraid, but we should be brave in the presence of our Lord. I was not afraid that day with my mom next to me. And just think, God was with my mom, the bunny, and me that day too.

Day 24

The Day

"This is the day the Lord has made; we will rejoice and be glad in it."

Psalm 118:24 (NKJV)

Please take a moment to read Psalm 118:20-24. As I studied these verses, I began to see a clear picture of Jesus. Verse 20 says, "This is the gate of the Lord through which the righteous may enter."

1. What does Jesus call Himself in John 10:9?

The psalmist then says in Psalm 118:21, "I will give you thanks, for you answered me; you have become my salvation."

2. Write Acts 4:12 below.

(Please hold your place in Acts while we glance back at Psalm 118.)

The next part of the psalm tells us that "the stone the builders rejected has become the cornerstone" (Psalm 118:22).

3. According to Acts 4:11, who is the cornerstone?

In ancient buildings, the cornerstone was the main stone placed on the corner of the structure. It was the foundational stone, and it was usually the largest and most perfect of all the stones. Jesus, of course, is the cornerstone on which the church is built.

4. What makes you glad about the Lord's salvation?

"The Lord has done this, and it is marvelous in our eyes."

Psalm 118:23

Each day we can rejoice in His salvation and love. Even, and perhaps especially, when difficulties arise, we always have God. He alone is our gladness and reason to rejoice. He gives the day purpose. At times it may seem like there is little in which to be glad, but as we focus on the Creator and Savior, we will discover that our joy is in Him.

Day 25

Hold the Hours

"Show me, Lord, my life's end and the number of my days;
let me know how fleeting my life is."

Psalm 39:4

My grandma used to say that time seemed to speed up as she got older. As I've reached middle age, I also find this to be true. Perhaps it's God's way of getting our attention. David wrote in Psalm 39:4, "Let me know how fleeting my life is." As we see how time flies, how the hours of our lives pass by so quickly, we can either get caught up in the cares of the day or we can hear the call of God to draw near to Him. As we grow older, it seems logical that we should grow closer to the Lord.

1. How do you see the rest of your life? What are your dreams or goals?

When I was little we used to sing "He's Got the Whole World in His Hands" in nursery school. I loved the part that says, "He's got the little bitty baby in His hands." As unsettled as the world has become, one might question whether He does have the whole world in His hands. It is overwhelming to think of the billions of people on the earth. Each one has needs, has cares, and is desperate to fill their life with God, whether they know it or not.

Hours can be spent doing so many different things: eating, sleeping, working, studying, cleaning, playing, watching, listening, talking, and the list goes on and on.

2. How does God fit into your hours?

3. How do you fit into God's hours?

We will finish today with a couple of verses from a prayer written by Moses. You may like to pray it too:

> "Teach us to number our days, that we may gain a heart of wisdom.
> Satisfy us in the morning with your unfailing love,
> that we may sing for joy and be glad all our days."

Psalm 90:12, 14

Day 26

Paint a Rainbow

"Whenever I bring clouds over the earth and the rainbow appears in the clouds, I will remember my covenant between me and you and all living creatures of every kind."

Genesis 9:14-15

1. According to Genesis 9:12-13, who sets the rainbow in the clouds?

2. Who does the rainbow belong to? Fill in the blank below.

"I have set _____ rainbow in the clouds…."

Genesis 9:13

We have used the image of the rainbow so freely that one would assume it belongs to people. If you think about it, the rainbow represents different things to different cultures. I remember when T-shirts with rainbows were popular in the 1970s and 80s. But regardless of what humans tend to think of the rainbow, or even how they use its image, the fact remains that it belongs to God.

I remember when I learned the colors of the rainbow. There are seven, which just happens to be the number of completion: red, orange, yellow, green, blue, indigo, and violet. I remember wondering, "What on earth is indigo?" Well, I've since learned that it is a dark purplish-blue. That's why it fits so well in between blue and violet.

3. What is your favorite color in God's rainbow?

If you have ever been through a difficult time, then you may be able to imagine how Noah and his family felt. They were tucked away inside the ark with all kinds of animals while the waters increased on the earth. For forty days the rain kept coming. When it was finally over, Noah and his family probably never wanted to experience a flood again.

4. What was the covenant that God made with Noah, his sons, and every living creature? You will find the answer in Genesis 9:11.

Whenever we experience rain, we can know for certain that it will eventually end. There will never be a flood that destroys all life again. The rainbow is God's beautiful sign of that promise.

"He who promised is faithful."

Hebrews 10:23

Day 27

Seas Calm

"You will keep in perfect peace those whose minds are steadfast, because they trust in you."

Isaiah 26:3

One summer's day when I was young, my family and I were out on Lake Sylvia in Minnesota. It was a beautiful day. We packed a lunch and planned to spend several hours on the boat. All of a sudden, practically out of nowhere, dark clouds moved in and it began to storm. We pulled up the anchor and headed back to the cabin as quickly as possible. My uncle was waiting for us. He grabbed a hold of my little hand, but I was not strong enough. I flew off the boat and cut my leg on the dock. I was alright, though.

When we visited the Sea of Galilee, the story I just shared with you went through my mind. I imagined what it must have been like when Jesus and His disciples were out on the boat when the storm hit. Jesus had fallen asleep on a cushion in the back of the boat. His disciples woke Him up and said, "Teacher, don't you care if we drown?" (Mark 4:38).

1. Please take a moment to look up Mark 4:39. Write it below.

The New King James Version says, "Peace, be still!" (I really love this version of this verse.)

2. Next, write down the names of Jesus in Isaiah 9:6. There are four.

    a)

    b)

    c)

    d)

Storms not only rage around us; sometimes they rage within us. We have been rescued, however, by the Prince of Peace! God made a way for us to be at peace with Him through His Son, Jesus. And the fruit of peace, found in Galatians 5:22, is available to all of God's children by the Holy Spirit. Just as Jesus calmed the storm in Mark 4, so He can calm the storm within you.

3. What kind of life does God want you to live? See 1 Timothy 2:2.

"Do not be anxious about anything, but in every situation, by prayer and petition, with thanksgiving, present your requests to God. And the peace of God, which transcends all understanding, will guard your hearts and your minds in Christ Jesus."

Philippians 4:6-7

Day 28

Things are Done

"Lord, you have been our dwelling place throughout all generations. Before the mountains were born or you brought forth the whole world, from everlasting to everlasting you are God."

Psalm 90:1-2

The Hebrew word *olam* means "old," "ancient," "long duration," "forever," or "eternal." One of God's names is *El Olam,* which means "God Everlasting." We see the Everlasting God in Psalm 90:1-2. It couldn't be more beautifully stated than verse 2: "Before the mountains were born or you brought forth the whole world, from everlasting to everlasting you are God."

1. According to Psalm 119:89, what is eternal?

Life changes. People move. Jobs come and go. Loved ones die. The Bible even says that Heaven and Earth will pass away (Mark 13:31). But, rest assured, there will eventually be a New Heaven and a New Earth (Revelation 21:1).

2. What will never pass away? See Mark 13:31.

The Word of God is so important because it is eternal. So many things have a beginning and an end. They can slip through our fingers like a handful of sand. But the Word—God's words—will always be with us.

3. What did the psalmist do with God's word in Psalm 119:11?

4. Why did he do this?

God lets us know when things are done. He helps us release them to Him. He comforts us through the process and gives us strength for a new day. He forgives our sins. We can hear from God through His written Word. What a treasure to find eternity in Him!

5. We will finish today with one final verse. Please take a moment to fill in the blank.

"Jesus Christ is the same yesterday and today and _____."

Hebrews 13:8

Day 29

You Are

"I will exalt you, my God the King;
I will praise your name for ever and ever.
Every day I will praise you and extol your name for ever and ever.
Great is the Lord and most worthy of praise;
his greatness no one can fathom."

Psalm 145:1-3

One morning I was putting nuts outside for the animals when I began to sing a new song to the Lord. The first verse came as I placed the seeds in the feeders. The second and third verses arrived a few weeks later. And this is how the song goes:

You are God

You are great.

You are kind.

You are loved,

the Lord divine.

Faithful, True,

that is You.

You are God.

In the wind,

in the rain,

You are calm

throughout the day.

Strength and love

from above,

You are God.

You are wise.

You are King.

You are right

in everything.

Lion, Lamb,

the great I AM,

You are God.

God is so many things to us. In this study we have seen Him as our Abba Father. I believe it will take a lifetime of learning to understand the fullness of who He is. Even in Heaven we will continue to learn about the glorious splendor of His majesty. Until then, embrace each characteristic of God as He reveals Himself to you. He is great. He is kind. He is loved, the Lord divine.

Please take a moment to write to God. Tell Him what He means to you.

"One generation commends your works to another;
they tell of your mighty acts.
They speak of the glorious splendor of your majesty—
and I will meditate on your wonderful works.
They tell of the power of your awesome works—
and I will proclaim your great deeds.
They celebrate your abundant goodness
and joyfully sing of your righteousness."

Psalm 145:4-7

Day 30

Your Psalm

He will rejoice over you with singing.

Zephaniah 3:17

I took some liberty with the last line in the poem "Daddy's Little Girl." It says, "I am Your psalm." Ultimately, God is our song. The psalms are sacred songs. They are songs of praise to the Lord our God. As we read the psalms, we see God's presence in people's lives. We see moments of fear and times of faith. We hear of brokenness and restoration. There is a shout of praise and a cry of despair. This is life in the psalms...and God is with us every step of the way.

1. Which psalm is your favorite? Why?

Psalm 23 is special to me for so many reasons. My mom gave me a book on this particular psalm many years ago. We discussed it in detail, so it is probably the one psalm that I truly understand. It was also included in my mom's funeral since it meant so much to us both. If you asked me which line I like the best, it would be difficult to choose. They are all so good, but perhaps verse 6 speaks the most to me right now: "Surely your goodness and love will follow me all the days of my life, and I will dwell in the house of the Lord forever."

Children live in their parents' house. We, as God's children, will live in our Heavenly Father's house forever. I rest in knowing that my mom is there right now.

2. What does Jesus tell us about His Father's house in John 14:2?

Until the day arrives when we finally see God face to face, we can know that His goodness and love are with us all the days of our lives.

Funny enough, I have a theory about growing old. For those who are in Christ Jesus, I believe the last day of our life could potentially be our youngest day. Some of the oldest people I know are really the youngest.

"Even youths grow tired and weary, and young men stumble and fall; but those who hope in the Lord will renew their strength. They will soar on wings like eagles; they will run and not grow weary, they will walk and not be faint."

Isaiah 40:30-31

I have heard a number of people refer to God as "Daddy." You would think by the title of this study that I, too, would have called my Heavenly Father by this name. But I haven't, not yet, not even in my most personal of prayers. Perhaps a part of me is still concerned that it isn't respectful enough. Perhaps I'm not childlike enough yet. One day, however, I hope that as I take my last breath my final prayer will be, "I'm coming home, Daddy. Your little girl will see You soon."